CLOSE TO HOME

Also by Frances Wilson

Where the light gets in
(Poet and Printer, 1992)

Frances Wilson

CLOSE TO
HOME

Beverley,
with very best wishes,
from Frances

May 1997

Rockingham Press

Published in 1993
by
The Rockingham Press
11 Musley Lane,
Ware, Herts
SG12 7EN

British Library Cataloguing-in-Publication Data

A catalogue record for this book
is available from the British Library

ISBN 1 873468 14 8

Printed in Great Britain
by Bemrose Shafron (Printers) Ltd,
Chester

Printed on Recycled Paper

Supported by the **Eastern Arts** Board

For all my family

Acknowledgements

Some of the following poems appeared first in the pages of Acumen, Envoi, Fat Chance, Foolscap, Iron, The Literary Review, Other Poetry, Outposts, Poetry Durham, Poetry Review, The Rialto, Slow Dancer, Smiths Knoll, Spokes, Staple, The Times Literary Supplement, Writing Women, and other magazines.

"Making Poppy Dolls" was awarded second prize in the National Poetry Competition in 1990. "Silence" won first prize in Orbis Rhyme International competition in 1991

Eight of these poems appeared in the pamphlet collection "Where the light gets in", published by Poet & Printer in 1992.

Front cover: *'Summer Night' by Harry Wilson,*
by kind permission of Mr. and Mrs. W. Neal.

Contents

I Could Live Here

No point pretending I don't know
what's hidden under the municipal tarpaulins
in all the carparks of this small town
where I've lived for thirty years.

But now they're lifted, I could be
in Cornwall, Wales, or any of those places
picked to slip to from the motorway
for a quick pub lunch, where we *Paid
and Displayed* and discovered — you remember?
a churchyard with a fallen angel,
almshouses in a perfume garden,
that covered market where you bought me
those earrings I still wear.

And it's with such holiday anticipation
that I fumble through what might be foreign
currency for a ten pence piece, and set off,
marvelling at the intricacy of the balcony
behind the library, the mustards and russets
of the wavering roofs, the bravado
of chimneys, that curve of street which leads
the eye to the tempting green of a park.

And I know, for one of those brief moments
of certainty, that I could live here,
in that room behind the irregular window
above the neon of the late-night grocer;
or that turret glimpsed between archways.
Or even up these steps, where low sun
through laburnum maps strange lines
on a familiar door, I could live here.

Almost

It's the scent I notice first —
peppery, waxy. Hawthorn in October?
Hardly. But autumn deals out these
almosts like aces; plays tricks.

There's a bush, quivering,
and a sound like a fridge
from the next room — it's ivy
flowerheads, humming with bees —

wings, stamens, pollen,
a powdery aura. Of course. Now
I recognise the animal odour. Honey.
I'm almost shy as I step closer

to examine these sunbursts of umbels,
molecular structures, each calyx
peeling back pale jade petals
to expose a nipple sticky with nectar.

No wonder the downy bodies are oblivious
as babies, intent on this moment
of sweetness. And I'm hot, almost
as if I'd watched something erotic.

Interior with Oranges

I wanted the house to myself
but now you're not here I can't settle,
pace rooms, hoping to be disturbed.

It's the oranges which stop me.
From half way down the stairs, a lamp
left on composes a corner of a room
into an *Interior With Oranges*.
They burn in their black bowl
on a lilac cloth beside olive
curtains. Outside, twigs of holly
scratch themselves against a wedge
of fence, imply a garden off-stage
where the light is barely credible.

But it's the oranges I look at.
From here the door-frame chops off
tops of curtains, windows, halves
a sofa, table, rug. My jacket,
slack on the back of a chair,
is mostly hidden. Abstract shadows
fold across an angle of wall.
Except for the oranges, everything
merely suggests the rest of itself.

It is a room glimpsed at night
from a fast train, awaiting completion,
needing a seated figure, reading.

A1

For me it's the A1, going north, cruising at 80.

Maybe it's because it's not quite a motorway
but broken by roundabouts, places which lure you
to picnic — Eaton Socon, Dry Doddington;

maybe it's because we're always on holiday
so we love every landmark — how the fields
flatten out between Huntingdon and Grantham,
the steep green curve where the slow Don passes,
the first slag heaps, the first smoking chimneys;

maybe it's Shostakovich and the warmth inside
the car's closed windows which insulates us
into this intimacy, so that I remember

how, starting at Peterborough,
you explained the basic principles
of electricity before we reached Leeds;

how at Melton Mowbray you remembered the pies
you ate as a child, Uncle Charlie who never made it
to fireman, who smelled of engines except on Sundays
when he wore spats; Aunt Mable with ideas above her station;

how once, speeding into the long bend beyond Sandy
where the road snakes and drops like a helter skelter,
a glimpse across long evening shadows of a church,
its feathery trees spread round a clutch of roofs,

was so perfect that I cried out "Look!"
And you did. And for a second I was sure
we'd crash. And it didn't matter.

It Seemed Like Peace

It wasn't the first time we'd been back
hoping to find the view we'd glimpsed only
in passing. We'd found the giant hogweed
where I'd had the cows eating out of my hand,

but somehow missed the turning, never found
the stretch of upland already composed for drawing.
But here it was. It seemed an omen, finding
the place at last, and just as we remembered —

that slow pull up a hill, a row of trees,
the road low between banks. And then
the laid-out landscape on our left, smooth
undulations like an endless eiderdown.

Nothing abrupt or dark. Chalk powdered hollows
which were barely shadowed. Just an occasional
fuzz as a hedge heaved itself over a ridge.
A wood on the horizon like mossed stone.

This time we parked, with the view framed
in the windscreen. Nothing passed. It's not
a road you'd take. Only a small wind bumped
against the car as if it wasn't looking.

It seemed like peace — the soft scratch
as pencils sketched the same lines separately;
an affirmation, mapping indentations, defining
horizons flat out under sun gone suddenly in.

I faltered, felt your hand beside me
pause. Stubble glittered like a trickle of oil.
Huge barrage balloons of cloud closed in, as shadow
after shadow after shadow advanced across the fields.

Downfall

I

Our plum tree's on its knees,
trunk snapped, top branches ground
into the grass, one flung out as if
to break its fall. Not even lying down.
It looks unseemly, like a botched job.
There must have been a struggle.

Huge as the house and older
than the century, when we moved
here it lorded it over the lawn.
In time it stooped a little lower,
leaves grew more wrinkled, blossom
sparser. Yet still the plums came, magenta-
black, each summer somehow sweeter.

And it gave more than food: beguiled
our babies with the shift of leaves;
played crocodiles with its bark;
supported cats, lodged birds,
gave houseroom even to parasites
which sapped its strength and left
their graffiti on the silk
parchment underneath its skin.

We put off clearing up. It seems
indecent. Strangers should lay it out,
box it for us to burn. Oh then
we'll mourn. But we're not ready
yet to face our lack of landmarks,
how the sky's grown cold
without its fingering of twigs.

II

It's taken us days to do it, to snip twigs,
lop branches, saw up the trunk. A hundred
times I've trudged down lugging the logs
from where the plumtree fell. The lawn's
lit up with flakes of buttered sunlight
like litter from a mammoth breakfast picnic.

But now the log-pile's stacked, each piece slotted,
packed precisely, firm as a dry-stone wall.
Though no lichen was ever this colour. Each cut
cross section shows a different map. Glows.
Raw umber, ochre sands surround a thin lead line
which edges beaches, inlets of each coral island.

And they'll soon lose sheen. But now they're whorls
of amber, pure as the song of the wren who through
the elder pours out his solo to the sky's clerestory.

Birth of a Drummer

He first came to his senses, as it were,
under the rippling of the plum tree's leaves,
against white sky so taut with heat
the hollow boom of planes was no surprise.
Sometimes his mother fed him out of doors.

He'd wake to bird sounds, more like morse
than songs, a syncopated tapping, riffs
of clear notes repeated and repeated, doves
soft vibrations. Plump in his pram, already
his fingers plucked and pummelled at the air.

Heron

For weeks she's turned a deaf ear to the football rattle
in the garden, the panic of sparrows. But this is different.
Overhead, four rooks are mobbing a heron. It's a bit of sky-
theatre, the way the rooks manoeuvre, the heron wheels,
his legs an encumbrance, his neck askew, a coathanger
holding a flapping grey bundle, twisting and twisting.

She remembers a shallow river with willows, how a piece
of shadow took off as she watched — that strange slow flight
swimming the bodyweight upward through silence and sunlight.
She thinks of small ponds, how it is days before the few
fish left flicker back to the surface; of the bully
beaten up in the playground who hanged himself later.

Yet she can't stop watching, though she wants to shout out
or find something to clatter, to stop it all happening.
But they're moving off anyway, over the rooftops,
a tangled mobile broken loose, growing smaller and smaller.
For a while she stays looking up, neck aching, waiting for something -
that clap of thunder you never hear after the final flash of lightning.

Twitching

I have reservations
about the nature of birds.
I suspect they're fabrications,
something a computer thought up.

Songs? Hardly. Scrambled
scraps. Imitations. Think
of the cuckoo, the rusty scrape
of a quail. A magpie's clack.

Just listen to that lark
winding itself up. From the hedge
the squeak of a soft toy.
Crank of a distant pheasant.

Incomplete sounds, squeezed out.
A clockwork cockcrow runs down.
Leather is wiped on glass.
There's interference on some radio.

And watch the way they strut,
hop, jerk their heads, stop
abruptly, not working properly,
take off at a tangent

whirring mechanically, drop
like a balloon let loose. Or flap
huge wings along unswerving lines.
Paper sculptures, plywood replicas.

It's beyond our furthest flights
to guess what will be set in motion
once the right key's punched,
their programme perfected.

That wren, once it's got the song
it keeps repeating right, and managed
to get it finished, will produce
music we've never even dreamed of.

Keeping Safe

She walks to the sea's edge, bracing herself
for that first chill shock. Only two children
are left, who race off, stick arms flailing
as waves smoke and flatten towards them.
A dog near the rocks is barking and barking.

It seems the tide's on the turn. And she wants
to mark it, do something to ease the emptiness.
From the litter she picks up a plastic cup,
and where the last sea reached, scoops sand,
turns out towers, one for each of the family;

then squats on her heels as first one rogue
wave then another surrounds them. Two towers
shift and start crumbling. She was mistaken.
This place is unsafe. It's the wrong moment.
And now she's scrabbling in panic to dig

a moat, to pile a wall on the sea's side.
And it matters to do it precisely, to pack
the sand smoothly, outer bulwarks sloping;
with the tide, a movement, a roar, a crowd
at her back. But no wave disturbs her.

So she watches till he calls from the cliff
path where he's sketching. Then she turns away,
climbs up to join him, relieved, mocking herself,
a grandmother alone on a beach, building defences.
Wiser to leave, to drive home without knowing.

First Walk of the Holiday

From indoors, through low windows, the views
here are skyless, intimate, close up against
slopes. I imagine walking, watching my feet.

Outside, distance returns. Clouds are bleeding
into the hills. I read the banked up, damped
down signals. Rain. Leaves turn their backs.

So I keep to the trail, the security of stiles.
Bracken uncoils. Ferns creep up stones, foxgloves
breathe out bees. I watch for snakes,

and follow the call of water, not the wind,
drop down to stepping stones, an obvious clue,
cross to a field invisible from the house.

And suddenly the sun shines here and nowhere
else, bleaching the bones of trees and boulders
sleeping in the turf. Sheep, in on the secret,

are nervy, clear off. I turn, expecting
to see someone arriving, but there's only me
and the wind and a brown bird I don't recognise.

So I climb back up, aware of absences, and fill
the kitchen with the smell of coffee. But no-one
stoops, scraping his boots, to enter the back door.

Intimacy

I came to paint the view,
that glimpse through the gap
of a gash of rape across folds of blue
and bluer fields which dissolve finally
into the misty cleft of the sea.

Then the shock of two sheep by the gate.
The rest of the flock, further off,
graze on, while these two stare, appalled.
I sense I have intruded on some intimacy,
drop my gaze, hitch up my shoulder strap,
while they, mistresses of rumination,
just stand until, initial scrutiny over,
one ambles off, the other one resumes
deliberate circular chewing.

While I, needing to draw to know,
now sketch her haughty profile, the curve
of her haunches, the hollow behind her shoulder.
Shorn, she reveals her aristocracy. Neat feet
beneath trim ankles balance her bulky belly,
her swaying walk. And she's not disconcerted
to be caught with muddied knees, her grubby rump
barely covered by her ridiculous stump of tail.

No, I'm the one embarrrassed by the exposure
of her bulging udder dangling its rosy teats between
splayed legs, who look away feeling the rub
of my own nipples in the heat beneath my thin shirt.
And even though she now drops her blunt head
and starts her cropping, not for one second
does she stop watching, casually yet precisely,
the way her lips nuzzle the short grass,
tease out the tenderest, missing nothing.

Sorting the Socks

I've you to thank for this,
how I slip my hand inside each sock,
feeling for holes, for weaknesses,
turn them inside out, smoothing,
tuck them into each other.

Year in, year out. You seemed
fulfilled by every day, yet in the end
lonely, an old machine still functioning
though the landscape's changed
and everyone's moved on.

The other day, feeling a tight
fuse smouldering, I stopped
before it reached anger, left
your son to turn his own socks,
a bid against obsolescence.

I'd hoped for freedom, but felt
faithless, as if I'd cut myself off
from all you'd shared with me —
repairing, taking care, knowing inside
is where it rubs. Rib against skin.

I thought of your hands
that last morning, plucking
out of the air invisible threads,
as if you'd discovered a new design,
or were tidying loose ends, finishing off;

while the sky beyond the window
began to peel back and show silver,
show willow and lilac's excited tugging,
birds clutching top branches.
Such a marvellous day for drying.

Facing South

So, the party's over. All that green anticipation,
summer's good times. Judging by this morning's evidence,
autumn was wild. The garden's still hung over.
There's litter everywhere. Wadges of soggy cobwebs,
burnt out dahlias. A single rose still smoulders,
the odd chrysanthemum flares. Crumpled leaves
stick to the shag-pile lawn, where something's smeared.

There is a fungal smell: bruised fruit, warm flesh.
Post coital. Leaf-mould mulched with wine.
A trace of last night's smoke stirs up a residue
of shame or longing. Or boredom. Nothing's clear.
Disappointments blur. Unfallen quinces gleam.
Perhaps it was almost perfect after all.

This is November. You veer from thinking
how you might have spent the time to wishing
it wasn't over. You hang around. Nostalgia's
safe, but rots. Look, frost has cleared the air,
sluiced down the sky. It's time to leave.
The last arrows are still pointing south.

Getting the Message

At dawn, six doves were in the rigging
of my mother's willow. That was the night
she dreamed of numbers, woke and groped in
to ask me who I was. When I left she knew,
but didn't seem to care, just stared
through me, stiff with concentration
on some calculation. I didn't count.

I chose the by-pass, needing speed.
Tarmac was lilac, pearl. Raw silk.
Hissed as I tore along. Something white
flapped against the windscreen. A bird
trapped in the wipers? A handkerchief?
A crossword giving the solution?
I couldn't stop. Whatever it was broke

loose over the meads, took off, tugging
at memory. Maybe that untied the knot
inside me, just as the grey serge sky
grew thin enough for the sun to light
a fan of gulls which glinted like glass
exploding in slow motion, showing
how time breaks before the heart drops.

Bathing my Mother

You hang back, call me
cruel, assure me you'll fall,
promise impossible behaviour,
anything to avoid that one step
into the treachery of white.

Years ago my baby daughter
would list implausible excuses —
a wobbly tooth, a hurting finger,
because her teddy said so —
to escape the ordeal of water.

Once in, of course, you're soothed,
though you won't admit it, fiddle
with bubbles while I soap your skin —
so thin, but soft as a child's —
fumble into intimacies,

glad of steamed-up glasses.
Wrapped in a warm towel, later,
you punish me with stiff
resistance, as I pat talc
into your shrunk hollows,

my belly tight, braced against
your slight weight, your need,
your terror, my fury, a longing
which takes my breath away
for another baby I'll never bear.

Cure

Knowing she's watching me shell peas
I can't believe her thumbs don't prick
to pick up a fat pod. How can she resist
surrender to this fist-sized, sleek-
bellied seal, the sheer feel of it?

I'd like to see her put it to her cheek,
cool as a closed mouth. When we were ill
she'd stoop and kiss our foreheads. Hands
were too crude, she said, held their own
heat. Only lips told the true temperature.

Once she'd smelled its grassy freshness
she'd have to press it open, loosen the peas
to patter into the collander; slip in
one green forbidden pill — risk just this
once the sweet she always denied herself.

Endings

I wanted my mother to fight.
I wanted people to say, How splendid!
How indomitable — at ninety still loving
her grandchildren, her garden, The Guardian,
still dismissing slipshod thinking,
split infinitives. I wished she wouldn't
yield so easily, wouldn't stay upstairs
waiting to die, while downstairs
I'd listen to her tread from bed to window
to commode to bed, scraping thin skin
from new potatoes, staring into the murky water.

But I wanted my cat to go quietly,
to uncurl obediently from my lap, acquiesce
to the cat basket, to my right to save him
from suffering, myself from having to witness
his plucky, undignified failure to leap
onto the boiler; not summon up this
last ferocity, not fight, his old self,
ears flat, eyes wide, howl, scratch
all the way to the vet; to leave me
prising open tins with our faulty opener,
ears still half pricked for his silent arrival.

Botticelli Baby:

a postcard to my mother

Mother, this one's for you.
Not the usual pastoral
back-drop, this inner city yard,
but the sun's pure Umbrian
and the street beyond with slopes
of rooftops, lines of washing,
is an exercise in perspective.

Look at the gold-leaf burnish
on the dark hair of the sun-browned
woman, her face a perfect oval;
bare-footed, black skirt
hitched up above her knees,
she sweeps the stones between
her pots of basil, bay, geraniums.

I'm sitting on the top step
stringing beans, thinking of you,
wishing you knew how much more often
since you died, I get in touch.
Remembering — missing now —
your English awkwardness,
how bad you were at kissing,

how you disliked garlic, mistrusted
herbs and music. Anything operatic
was beyond your repertoire. You
couldn't have been less Latin. And yet
you'd drop your maiden name *Tarelli*
into conversations with the proud
deliberate frequency of a lover's.

Look where your lineage has reached.
See how your grand-daughter props
up her broom, loosens her skirt,
stoops and scoops from beneath
the fennel's feathery shadow
her plump and dimpled baby,
Italian as any Botticelli cherub.

The Envelope

It's not her effects in our house —
her sideboard, her clock, her chair,
not even her favourite amber
necklace I now wear.

It's an envelope in the drawer
beside my bed, my name
in her looped, sensible hand,
shaky, but still the same.

And it's not the new loss I feel,
it's the old eight-year-long ache
that only her letters soothed —
nights when I'd lie awake,

days when my best friends
kept whispering with each other —
that bottomless homesickness
when I missed my mother.

1st. February

Where the road's up, in vans
workmen hug the last fug
of breakfast and *The Sun*
behind steamy windows.

While outside's a picture
beaten in bronze and pewter.
Tarmac's salted with frost.
Grass has a silver finish.

But January has clanged shut.
There's defiance about.
Pollarded limes punch upward,
willows streak gold.

And toddlers, fists clenched
in mitts, bears strapped to backs,
stomp well ahead of prams
and mums, under yanked-down hats.

Grandfather's Game

Up rough tweed, over steep
rock with no foothold was
the way to my grandfather.

I could barely see the top.
His mouth was a fissure,
his eyes fathomless.

But I knew his laughter,
how everything quaked.
I could smell danger.

Even under the table
the tips of his landslide
would reach my white arms.

Grandmother couldn't help me,
scuttled out of sight
to the shelter of her kitchen.

It was my task to climb —
only to the plateau of his knees,
I never reached his heart —

where I waited long enough
to get a taste for safety
before the ground gave way.

Bruised, at his feet,
I would begin again. I'd never
give in to him, give up.

I'd not be one of his 'pretty
girls' who clucked to his call
and lost their heads.

Launch

I might have been a paper boat,
his launch was so soft I'd hardly
feel his touch, just a rush of air
then the drop back to where he stood
behind me. And he stopped pushing
once I'd learned to lean my weight
into the swing's movement, catching
each arc at the turn to force it higher.

Until I reached almost horizontal,
could see into our neighbour's garden —
a terrace, hidden from our upstairs
windows, a pond I'd just glimpsed bits of,
squinting along the fence — and beyond,
a world wider than my snailtrails,
whatever mystery was lost replaced
by a new mysterious restlessness.

But best of all was to slip out late,
after supper in summer, my nightie
instantly damp round my ankles,
for that leap in the dark, guessing
the exact spot on the swoop up to let
go, so that the swing's momentum
shot me off. Aware he was near by
somewhere, smoking his last pipe.

Grandmother's Goitre

It was less the goitre itself that obsessed me
than its inappropriateness — far too fleshy
an excrescence for so bony a lady —
too round and jolly behind its velvet
choker, its brooch her only ornament.

It was never referred to, though it bobbed
each time she swallowed. I couldn't not look.
So I scoured books for pictures, reconstructed
her fifteen minutes of glory: in the spotlight
with a golden ball (I knew all the stories) —

a princess in austere black taffeta watered
with sequins — her sea-lion performance.
I could see she had poise. And already I'd learned
how quickly success can slip through one's fingers,
could imagine the shock, that moment of horror

as the ball stuck in her throat. Like a light
going out. I never asked. I feared the truth
might dislodge something for ever. I kept watch
while she had her nap; held the chair as she reached
to take down the best china. But she never faltered.

Making Poppy Dolls

Finding them's easy — the excitement's
in the heat of the long afternoon, the smell
of tar — because they're common enough,
shove their way between ranks of orderly corn
at the field's edge, line up along roadsides,
flaunting scarlet. They're asking to be picked.

But once you're down in the sour grass
beside them you see they're fragile, teetering
on tall stalks, their silk still creased —
mothwings emerging. For a second you pause before,
choosing the brightest, you fumble your fingers
right down where it's dark, to snap it off low.

Now it gets tricky. There's no way your sweat
won't do damage as you fold back each tissue petal
and pinch them tight into a neat waist so that the top
rounds out into a pert bust; as you twist the wide grass
sash to hold it all firm, taking pains with the knot
so that the blade won't break, leaving the head

exposed in its soft ruff. Now you want something
sharp, a few quick jabs, to prick the features.
Next, for a second leg, take a length of stem
and poke it up under the skirt, another through
the bodice for the arms, even if they always look
crucified, the eyes terrified, the mouth howling.

It could always be singing. Only it isn't.
And there's nothing you can do except lay them
in rows. Even the fizz of the wind through dry corn
won't lift their skirts now. And you're bored,
with nothing to show but dead flowers and red
smears on your fingers. And wishing you hadn't.

Treat

Just an old wood and the usual warnings
and lugging the picnics, put you off guard,

unprepared for the world upside down,
that first glimpse of sky on the ground.

More than anything else you wanted to scoop
up all that blueness, to take the shock home.

But when you splashed in, it paled, became
ordinary flowers, till you learned

the trick was to pick them keeping an eye
on the distance, a kind of horizon to steer by.

And there was something fishy about
how the stems slipped through your fingers,

at last slid out, naked and white,
like something owned up to. Much later,

after the leap-frog, the rounders
and biscuits, you all straggled back

down a path trampled with flowers, triumphal
arrival at the bus, where you sat on the lap

of a big girl who'd suddenly picked you,
who played with your plaits. And kissed you.

Back home you rushed in to your mother,
your limp armfuls of flowers reburnished

with this new shock. And for nights after
you'd lie awake, deliciously risking,

your worse nightmare — you were an orphan,
she was your mother, she'd have to bath you.

Lessons

No-one can change faster than I can
under a towel, behind a bit of wall —
drop a bra, slip into pants, allowing
no glimpse of private flesh at all.

No-one can write so secretly but so
discreetly — no vulgar fortress
arm to block out friends, although
I keep my words close to my chest;

or walk more skilfully the tightrope
between odd and ordinary so both
sides stay happy; nor lie so eloquently
without ever uttering an untruth.

No-one can cause more distractions
yet remain unnoticed; or eat more neatly,
elbows flush to the waist as wings;
or dispose of food so completely

undetected, into my lap, up sleeves,
or, if really cornered, merely drop it,
then with a pass a footballer would envy,
sidekick precisely under someone else's feet.

Waiting for 70°

For a week the swimming pool
would have been drained, repainted
electric blue, refilled. No water
ever looked cooler — while we sweated
in gingham and aertex, lolled in long grass
between the hard courts and the ha-ha
dreaming of diving, imagining satin
water slide off our thighs, performing
effortless crawl, arriving first
at the far end; the adrenalin rush
of popularity, better than the dizziness
of nicotine. Rumour smouldered
round the school like heath fires, long
before the lists went up, the announcement
in assembly. Only then came the real sounds
of summer — the muffled waterfall roar
of the filter from beyond the cedars; jungle
shrieks of girls, weird as macaws.

Mouse

Odd that she escaped our witch-hunts.
While others were excommunicated, burned
alive, she sidled through, half noticed;
buff-haired and sallow skinned, blurred

as if she hadn't hardened. She knew a trick
or two about invisibility. We wouldn't risk it.
In fact it was her mice. As if they wove
a spell round her. Round us. Up her sleeve,

this bulge. A sort of shiver. Where she sat
the air would grow electric, until Miss Smith
snapped: *"Madeleine, what are you playing with?"*
Then, gauche and cornered, she would pat

her blazer pockets, prod her tunic. No flicker
of a whisker. She never searched her knickers.
And naturally, we too adored our pets. Missed
our family spaniels madly. Loved cats. Kissed

pony pictures. Wept through Lassie Come Home.
But who'd be daft enough to want to stumble down
at night in the wet to a hut with a lock
which creaked, with scufflings at your back

and your torch growing thin? We shuddered
and sniggered indoors. Read stories. Later
she'd slide in from the dark, more of a shadow
than ever, yet trailing a hint of adventure.

As if she had broken bounds. Or worse,
knew something we didn't. Her final trick —
one summer term she simply didn't come back.
The one we all wanted to bring off, of course.

Revisiting the Pigs

Once you've checked the nails you hammered
last summer into the oak are holding,
and the sparrow's skull and bits of candle
are safely hidden, you slope off to see
if the pigs are still there. And they are,
doing all the things pigs are supposed to do —

snuffling and grunting and wallowing in mud
like log-jams, then heaving their overweight up
as if they'll never make it, to sit for a moment
amazed to be upright, before lumbering over
to look at you sidelong, whiskery, curious,
snouts like soft buttons, tails coming undone.

Surprise, reassurance, relief, that they
go on doing all this — as if you might find
last summer's best friend from next door
still wants to play the same games, isn't
wearing mascara, a sweater you'd be forbidden,
isn't ever so sorry, but she's just going out.

Looking for the Wolf

The first time, just the path to herself must have been enough —
so many flowers, the invisible cuckoo, a blueness sometimes
where the trees thinned, which might have been sea; and wind
lifting her hair and flattening the grass at the wood's edge
where shadows could have hidden anything ash-grey and shifting.

Though nothing happened, it would have been enough
to reach the snugness of her granny's cottage; to taste
toast with butter melting; on her fingers still a residue
of stickiness from the thick sap of bluebells and wild garlic,
leaving a scent she'd think of always, afterwards, as wolf.

But if she'd returned, like me, time after time, after
the encounter — all that excitement, but no bones broken —
might she not have found the wood empty, though seeing it all
still there — the wind making sunlight uncertain, secret orchids,
the ferns' strangeness? Wouldn't it have been worse, knowing

it was no longer enough, making her feel corrupt, her pulse
racing, briefly, only at the crows patrolling her journey?
Like me she'd have been relieved to see the woodcutter approaching,
balding a little, perhaps, but still wholesome; his six dogs, all
except one, let free to flatter her with indiscriminate enthusiasm;

his voice, as he restrained, carressed the cringing bitch,
explaining how she'd been mauled, how he'd undo the damage.
She too would have found quick tears blurring what might have been
a movement behind him; his smile, as he watched her accept
his hounds' fawning, staunching her hunger, like sucking a pebble.

The Invasion

Every two months the window cleaner lays
seige to my privacy. He scales my wall,
bangs his advancing pail, his whistle pries
into each room. I think of boiling oil.

I resent his weight against my windows,
his ladder, witness to my negligence —
my unmade bed, the milkbottles in rows —
even his seeming bland indifference.

For half an hour he makes me the intruder.
He's visible for all the world to greet,
while I creep furtively from shade to door,
like a voyeur who only watches feet.

And when he's gone I still step warily,
afraid to disturb this clarity within,
exposed, it seems, to more than scrutiny,
as if his rub had worn away my skin.

Watering her Neighbour's Plants

It feels like trespass. The key turns
awkwardly. The place can't be empty —
it was different before she entered.
She listens to the clock keeping time
with the quiet; slips off her shoes.

She's glad of the gush of the tap,
pads round the house on a treasure hunt
for plants which give no clues. If only
she could lip-read lilies. The rooms are full
of pictures which disappear as she nears them.

Upstairs she's warmer — something about
the untroubled beds, a scent of jasmine.
In front of a wardrobe she imagines herself
naked, looking along an avenue to a lake;
feels the sun on her ankle, soft as moss.

Back home she's shy, finds her own house
charming, a friend she's hardly seen.
She is shocked by signs of aging.
When her husband asks why she's been gone
so long, she covers his words with kisses.

Staying Away

You drink their coffee, unwilling
to seem different; slip up to bed
first, unsure of the house-rules;
think the bath-mat's your towel
till too late; hear them all
downstairs for hours, still talking.

Exhaustion fools you. Sleep keeps
jerking out of your reach. You're hot,
cold, count up to eight new aches,
discover how your heart-beat,
when you lie on your left, revs,
stops — you're dying — kick starts

to a regular pounding, louder
than a clock, their footsteps,
doors slamming; at last fills
the silence, the whole house,
as you creep to the lavatory,
not knowing the floorboards.

You need someone to kiss you
goodnight. You think of him
reading, his back to your absence;
how you used to imagine your mother,
listening to ITMA; her handwriting:
Darling, I'm so glad you're settling down nicely.

Chocolate Lover

There's something I must tell you about my black lover,
my old tom — it's how his mouth waters for chocolate.
The mere crunch of a wrapper will bring him from nowhere.
And you'd think I was edible, the way he drools over me.
One passing caress — and he's spooling saliva.

He likes me best horizontal, leaning back against cushions.
Then he'll stand on my chest, tease me into submission, rubbing
my cheek with his, thrusting his nose into my erogenous ears
in an ecstacy of needling, his eyes tawny, sexy, half closed
on his fantasies. I'm melted, lost in sensation. I'm his.

At last, with a lion's shake, he scatters his dribble, subsides
like a balloon on a field; shudders, flattens out along my body;
his head presses my breast, his breath feathers my throat,
the pulse of his purr and my heartbeat syncopate. His belly
against mine, the flutter of his flank is a child in my womb.

Watching a Cellist Playing Brahms:
sketch with reference notes

First, rough in the composition, how the light falls
from above; block in the edge, the audience,
attentive as stones, leaning towards the stage;
check tones, recessions, correspondences: how that curve
there is echoed there and there; how spaces become shapes.
Note how that shadow is more mauve, that one more ochre;
how the umbers, olives, in the abstract on the wall,
through half closed eyes glow but grow darker.
Remember: burnt sienna, prussian, indigo.

Now, notice how the light falls on the slim curve
of her arm, all I can see for the crowd; the small
steep wrist-bone, the cluster of white knuckles;
how it is thrown up, softer, from the polished floor,
an afterglow along the intimate underside, how it blooms
like candlelight in the secret hollow of her underarm;
see how delicately the bow, between her fingertips
and thumb, becomes an adder's head, dips and draws out
threads of song as fine as wire; or jams out sounds
more muscular than the pale arm which jabs and rears
and sways, then flicks a last few notes, like rain ending.

I think this is a poem I should have painted. But then
how should I have shown the window behind me open
onto a London evening garden? And would you have heard
the clear song of the blackbird pouring in from the dark,
catching the light, so that the Brahms lost focus, at the edge?

Roll-call

Really I hardly knew you. I sat at the back
of a church packed with men, minders who'd failed
to save you, trying to remember what you'd said
about God; imagining you prancing in elsewhere in red
high heels, announcing your unpronounceable name.

I never could spell it, never got used to the way
you'd waltz late into class in those improbable shoes.
Your glamour, anarchy, the way you mocked everything,
your sudden kindness — nothing quite fitted, until the time
we talked about death and you told us about the cancer.

Crossing Hungerford Bridge

It's always just stopped raining as I exit
at The Embankment, and the sun, pale as a moon,
glitters from the glass of the South Bank
complex, where I'm going, oils the surface
of the river where it coils around
the thick trunks of the railway arches;
and I take two steps at a time, leaping the sky
scattered on the tarmac, because it's so good
to be back, with passing trains setting
the whole world rocking — and I remember journeys,
foreign voices across midnight platforms,
and I could be young again, live rough —

so when at the turn to the bridge I see
between girders whose shadows you could frame
those spaces under arches with piles of boxes —
like the attic landing where I camped with toys —
I'm not so saddened by the couple crouched
behind a threadbare raincoat, whose notice
HUNGRY AND HOMELESS seems hardly different
from notes for biscuits I'd drop down the stairwell;
and it's easy to smile and toss coins into the hat
of the lad juggling beside the bright kiosk
before crossing the pavement to shoulder open
stiff doors onto the warm and carpeted interior.

It's always dusk and raining when I leave.
Trees drag slack skipping ropes of lamps
and trains move in too close; while the river
by the jetty doesn't seem to know which way
to go. But I do. Home — my bag weighed down
with books I've spent my cash on, so I'm glad
the juggler's gone. But where the couple sat
hunched together, a boy turns his face to the wall.
And in seconds I'm past, racing through the night
to my own lit windows. But I can't leave it alone,
can't leave it alone. Like a scab. Keep going back
to the bridge. And the dark. And it's always raining.

The Danger of Gardens

Make no mistake, this is a sun trap.
Look where light reflected from the window's
glass bleaches the privet's darkness.
Undeflected, it blazes into your skull.
Can you remember what you were thinking
only a moment ago? Can't you see,
that chalky azure flutter from flower
to flower is flaked off, blistered sky?

If you must enter, wedge the gate open;
avoid high walls, wisteria's papery grapes,
the hum of bees under pleached limes.
It is enchantment. You will be drowned
in the wind's hiss that this is paradise.
Quick, pick up the whiff of nicotine,
geranium scent of Sundays, a hint
of fox beneath the maytree's avalanche.

Don't fall for the scarlet sheen
which leads to the poppy's purple heart.
It is war paint. This is a jungle.
See how it has thickened overnight.
Stay too long and it will close in,
fatten you up with colour, scent, heat,
till you forget the way you came, the world
outside. Grow sluggish, drugged. Oblivious.

Silence

For months he dug, hollowing a cave of silence.
He knew what he wanted. This was his earth. The field
above was almost unaltered. You'd never believe
what it hid. Such darkness. And peace. It had been a shot
in the dark to move here, though he'd felt a gun
at his head for years, the trigger cocked. He'd lived

all his life in the house where his father had lived
all his life. It had seemed like an end, leaving the silence
of the still furnished rooms. Taking his father's gun
was an impulse, a game of a sort, making the field
a hideout for outlaws. He'd felt suddenly young. A shot
of such happiness stabbed him, he couldn't believe.

And now that he'd been there a year, what he couldn't believe
was why he'd not come before. How could he have lived
trapped between walls for so long, with his nerves shot
to shreds? Outside was an endless discovery of silence —
the voice of the wind in the poplars, the grasses. The field
was his world where he tended his plot and his dugout. The gun

was merely a barricade. But he grabbed up the gun
when a stranger appeared from the trees. He didn't believe
it was friendship. What letters? The postman avoided his field.
Everyone thought he was mad. Well, let them. He lived
here in peace, harmed no-one. Words were like grit in the silence,
bitter and hard. Shocking. Like biting on lead shot.

And the stranger retreated, uneasy, angry, but still shot
question after question over his shoulder. Was the gun
loaded? Where were his permits? After he'd gone, the silence
felt crumpled. He had to remake the morning, must believe
there had been no intruder, no harm done, that he lived
inviolate still in the intimate world of his field.

But nothing was ever the same. The breath of his field
was corrupted. Rabbits ran low as if someone had shot
one of their number. Birds sang in fragments. He lived
his nights on a knife edge, by day he cradled his gun
like a child in his arms, mouthing curses he didn't believe.
When the man came back, he watched him across the silence.

But when the gun went off, he couldn't believe
he had fired it, though the silence which filled the field
was as if he had shot every bird that had ever lived.

Another Letter to Gwen John

'... died 1939, in Dieppe, where she had gone for an unknown reason'
Catalogue: 1985

I did come, really. Please don't think
because I haven't written sooner that
I didn't care. I thought you knew.
Although, of course, with all the crowds ...
That was the problem. As it always is.

I saw it straight away. Something
familiar. The rooms, the light;
their hands, those letters. Yes,
it was recognition. Not like a mirror,
nor a photograph, but in my mind.

The kind of women we were taught to be.
Modest, not plain, patiently drawing
all the world's unrest into their laps.
'There is no higher aspiration, girls,
than to be of service to a worthy man.'

You set such an example. A model
prefect, one of the older girls
who wore devotion like a uniform
with subtle flair. Where you sat,
shadow and light were eloquent as doves.

Yet you revealed so little. The merest
hint, as if you'd just stopped smiling,
implied you'd not surrendered; made
one hope, one day, for unimagined
intimacies. No wonder women flocked.

So I held back, lost confidence.
Everyone talked about you. 'Oh, *yes,*'
they said, 'Gwen *John!*' as if they shared
the secret. Yet no-one seemed to know
about Dieppe. That, you took with you.

Understanding Rodin

In the afternoon art class
we're drawing each other.
Women who've come with friends
move closer together. In a corner
a fat man shrinks behind his easel.
His gratitude as I settle beside
him is humbling, how he offers
himself, shoulders awkward, shyly.

Just a faint scratch as charcoal
explores ears, coils into nostrils,
approaches the neat indentation
above his upper lip where my finger
would fit. Where the lips touch,
how private that line between closed
and open, how lovely this slack
curve's soft edge, his mouth.

And I understand Rodin, why he made
love to his models, having known them
in stone. Not to would have been
far more unfeeling. And no wonder
they went mad, wrote to him daily,
arranged the rooms where they waited
in pastels subtle as flesh for that
slow discovery of their own beauty.

Hybrid

These new tulips are shouting.
They are rapacious.
They gulp sunlight whole.

The old tulips are decorous,
upright as ramrods.
Sheathed
in the propriety of leaves
they unclench just enough
for bees to enter,
but shut up hunger,
hold anger in.

The new tulips have no shame.
They are all throat.
Wide open, they expose
ravenous linings of flesh,
offer everything.
Such abandonment
shocks.

Old tulips
go soft in the end,
lose their dignity,
expose parts
they've kept concealed,
keel over.
They are painful to look at.
It's hard to throw them away.

New tulips too
fall about finally.
But it looks more like
being dead drunk on sun
or an overdose of bees.
Or even laughter.

Looking the Other Way

'An old man lies dead, shot on his way
to feed his pigeons.' The photo shows
his face the wrong way up, coarsened
by newsprint. I stare until he blurs,

remember those faces I used to draw
in my rough book; and the time my lover
lay, his head in my lap, while I traced
each crevice of his up-side down loved face,

till everything at the edge bled out.
And nothing changed, but now I saw
a stranger, the way he looked at me,
unblinking upper lids, bottom lids

blinking upwards. Something reptilian,
sub-human. How could I trust that
blank expanse where mouth and nose
should be, where his hair became beard?

And all I wanted, for a fraction
of an instant, was to wipe him out, this man
innocently getting up to let the cat in;
setting off to feed his pigeons.

The Poetry Reading

Though the spotlight's on
him, he's up against shadows.
Under his tubular chair
a cat's cradle of shades
of gunmetal, dove, slate,
is stretched across a stage
as luminous and dangerously flat
as the sea under storm clouds.

While from the black outside
the blank windows comes
an endless thrumming, a million
billiard balls rolled down grooves
at the drop of a coin, a convoy
of distant tanks breasting
slope after slope and sinking.

It's skateboarders, swooping down
concrete sidewalks, weaving between
pillars, lovers, dossers, film buffs
and musicians — making their mark
on the dark with panache and flourish.
They know about balance and rhythm,
pushing risk to its limits, the line-
break which makes the heart leap.

Ms. X

every so often let her hair down
chez Michel, placed her neck
meekly on the basin's block,
throat sacrificial, eyes closed
waiting to feel his cool fingers
like fish nuzzling among fronds

kept six-monthly teeth checks
in a discreet victorian villa,
shady with laburnum; watched clouds
like slipless pillows; her head
brushing his chest, surrendered
to the narcotic taste of mouthwash

annually in the intimacy
of a darkened room, chanted letters
like a mantra, trying to get it right,
held her breath as his breath
touched her cheek, sensed his eye
behind his torch's pinprick, probing

every two years adventured
up to London, where she waited,
stripped to the waist in a room
like a Paris attic — view of rooftops,
pigeons in the gutter — for his hands
to press her breasts, exploring

in the High Street, passed
the undertaker (whom she'd taught
briefly) in shirt-sleeves, caught
a whiff of sweat; felt her heart
murmur; imagined being laid
out under his practised fingers.

Split Second

I'm carrying piles of ironing for airing.
Windows are wide open on an innocent morning

when out of the blue
comes a metallic nasal drone
drilling my eardrums, filling up the air —

a split second —

time for a shutter to fling back
on blackout, a cellar,
my sister's thin knees,
a tin box with buttons
and overhead
a ripening marrow slung in a string hammock,
a cartoon barrage balloon —

before the sick moment when the sound stops —

and in the sunny bedroom I'm rigid,
watch each step, inch open folds of curtain,
but find the bee clamped to a lampshade,
drugged, docile,

easy to clap in a mug
and let go.

Remembering Dandelions

You can keep rape, I'll stick to older gold:
dandelions, my childhood love. I longed
to be like them. Nothing kept them down.
They were common, unprotected, lived rough
at the road's edge. Felt the ground swell.

Their company was unspeakable — odd stockings,
bottles, opaque cast-offs I didn't understand.
They saw what happened after dark in secret
places at the back of fairgrounds, on rank
grass stretches. They knew what dogs sniffed.

Impatient for knowledge, I'd pick them
closed, prise them open, gaze into their
shaggy, brazen suns, too yellow to be true;
outstare each chipped tooth-petal, each
forked filament, until I blinked mauve.

Their leaves sent shivers through me. Still
do, from thick-fleshed spine to thin-veined
jagged membrane. I'd grasp them fiercely,
braced always against some snag, sting,
poison even, then watch the atavistic fins

grow limp, but give away nothing. Only their milk
left tell-tale smears, earth stains or worse
which wouldn't rub off. At bedtime my licked skin
still tasted bitter, smelled of pepper. All night
I'd toss, hot, knowing I'd played with fire.

Mascara

I should like to sing the praises of mascara,
those thumb-sized boxes with dry slabs of black
and a minuscule brush and a mirror.
A toy. A transition from childhood.

They opened up a glamorous initiation —
in a bedroom in a pension in Boulogne, by an American girl,
only fifteen, an Audrey Hepburn, innocent-sultry.

I remember the soft sweep of her brush,
gazing into my own eyes, wide against tears
as if one blink might blind me,
but worth it for the metamorphosis,
the familiar stranger who confronted me all evening
from every mirror, sophisticated, doe-eyed, dusky.

I remember the weight of my lashes,
a constant reminder, a subtle branding, a permit
for entry to tight jumpers, jiving, and the rest.

And for years after, whatever the outcome of an evening,
there was always that moment of invulnerable narcissism
late on my way to a party — the neat spit onto the caked block,
working up a muddy froth, then the careful strokes,
risking the sway, maybe, of a double decker bus —
to ease on the darkness, watching the transformation.

Mermaid and The Man

I warned you

I told you
not to drag me
from the slime.

So don't pretend
you don't know who I am.
Remember how your desire
fleshed out my song — that echo
down the caverns of the dark.
You loved me, then.
You thought me
beautiful.

Come, look again.
I'm not so bad now, am I?
Given time, you'll be surprised
what half truths you'll get used to.
Even the stink. Peel back my skin —
I'm only fish and blood.

Too late to throw me back.
Your fumbling in the muddy depth
has pulled some plug. The only water left
is in my shadow on this hard slab.
My body rocks itself.

Don't go.

You thought me up — I'm yours.
I'll be the shadow in your mirror,
the fingernails against your window in the night.

Second by second I am drying out.

Please   *Break the spell*   *Kiss me*

Loose

Back home, his meeting over
early, he called his lover
on the cordless phone
knowing she'd be alone.

Felt that electric stir.
While everywhere the air
was static with his desire
to have her here and here.

Then the insistent bell
(her voice still at his ear) —
a thin youth trying to sell
him useless householdware.

He told him to go to hell
and slammed the door. But first
caught, "Bastard, fuck you as well."
Knew she had heard him cursed.

Unsung Heroes

So, how about the innkeeper, how did he feel?
He was a nice guy too. He'd seen those shots,
the camps, the starving children.
Hadn't he had that jar of coins,
the Tarts and Vicars party?
He'd have been moved by all those wounds,
the callous passers-by;
he'd have stripped off his shirt
and lent his horse —
done the Samaritan bit.

But I wonder, how did it feel
when the Samaritan left,
leaving him lumbered?
It was he who had to run upstairs
at every whim of the imperious bell,
who had to titillate the appetite,
whose sleep was broken every night
by screams, the nightmare replay.
It was he who had to hear and hear again
the same old story of the robbery
trotted out to all the regulars
and any passing stranger,
washed down, no doubt, with beer.
A veritable Ancient Mariner —
he must have emptied the bar.

And not just for one compassionate afternoon,
but day after day after day
while trying to run his business.
And as the man grew fit and bored,
and began to brag and throw his weight about
and chat up servants, maybe even the wife,
the innkeeper must have found it hard
and wished he'd been the one to find the man
and get the praise, and had the cash
to hand him over to someone else's patience.

Common Ground:
Night Watch at Greenham

Across the ugliness of orbital London,
through the despondency of Slough,
along the endless miles of motorway
laying waste the fields,
we shed reluctance, eager now
to arrive. Welcome visitors,
we receive scant greeting.
No Judas kiss, no 'How's the family?
What weather for the time of year!
Do, please, sit down.'
No chat of this or that.
You are not here for this.

And nothing has changed.
Here is still the wire
fencing the vast enclosure
to keep us out, and to protect
the habitat of war. Between his fire
and shanty-hut the puppet tiger
still paces his small path
believing himself free.

Here is still the concentration
of lights searching your camps,
which lie between their hardware
and the software of uneasy affluence,
unchanged, ragged, domestic,
your litter of disorderly love
exposing their other awful orderliness,
reducing the too huge horror
to a definable, appalling truth.

No, nothing has changed. But we,
once again strangers, wait
on the perimeter of your intimacy,
self-effacing, hiding
our easy gifts brought to decorate
your barbed and spartan lives.
Until, at last, united by the night,
we lay down our small offerings
of love and guilt, the weighted diffusion
of our loyalties, and you share with us
your complicated single-mindedness,
and we find common ground.

Warmth

The time I was coldest was the night
they melted ice in a makeshift kettle
over their ramshackle camp-fire, to fill
hot water bottles to warm us as we watched
over them sleeping. Those were the days
of the cold war. I remember the cat
which slept in the small of my back
between layers of jumper and duffle,
while we tried to compile a crossword
for them to unravel. In the bleakest
hour it clawed its way round to my lap
and snatched my sandwich. How we laughed
at the string of objects hung across
a tree's fork, too cramped with cold
to get up and check it. At dawn they told us
it was a shrine, how her husband had loved her
enough to allow her almost to die there,
before gathering up their gortex, their wood
and kettles, ready to face the day,
the farce with the bailiffs. While we
hurried back to hot baths and central
heating, and a few days off from guilt;
our fear even, thawed somehow, briefly.

Juggling

Pick something which glitters. Don't be afraid
of sequins or lurex, things luminous. This is your sky.
These are your comets, your moons' transits.

Plant your feet till you're rooted, playing at being a tree.
Feel your weight drop until you're all buttock
and so still you can feel your own infinitesimal swaying.

Notice now the space around you, how it explores
your contours, defining your outline till
all you are is the place where the air ceases.

And you'll feel the ache in your shoulders swell,
then pour out at your fingers where the balls nestle
in your palms' hollows, wrists swing, loose sprung. Ready.

Though you're reluctant to spoil this stillness,
safe harbour — till you pick up — what is it?
a scent? a current? — and you're off and following,

fluent, easy, the balls completing, repeating
your arms' parabolas. And now it's all rhythm,
hands' small movements, colours multiplying themselves,

sparklers' afterflash drawing on darkness.
You're ground control, the mouth of a fountain,
each soft landing satisfactory as a boundary catch.

Till you switch off, sweating as if you'd been running,
head spinning; behind your lids pinpricks
of light as if you'd been miles away, star-gazing.

Coming of Age

Like boys at the first windfall
of conkers, spiders at the first frisson
of autumn, this June day's midsummer
sunshine has brought you out: old women

risking pastels, blatantly barelegged —
you, whose grandson years ago stuck up
my daughter's hair with playdough —
you, who used to drive me round

for Meals on Wheels, and knew each
name but always called me 'Florence' —
in shorts even! How you brazen out
aging, exposing varicose wirings,

melting ankles, bird-legs; how you dress up
your crowning glory's lack-lustre
with wild hats or dyeing or just waving.
Straight backed, defiantly driving,

or blocking access with zimmers,
shopping trolleys — inexorable as tanks,
you get your own back on skateboarders,
those youths who at night darken your doorways.

I'm not one of you yet, but as I wait behind
you in queues, you already acknowledge me
differently, recognise markings: the backs
of my hands, how I stand against sunlight.

And I catch your private humming, pick up
a sweetish brittle scent of something folded
inward; half glimpse beyond smudged lipstick,
runnels of eyeshadow, your small fierce glances,

your reedy intimacies, your painful optimism —
things I've also known and dreamed of, never told.
A kind of pollen count. O bright, brave,
indomitable old women, I'm coming, I'm coming.